Cause For Joy

A Book of Christmas Stories

Cause For Joy

A Book of Christmas Stories

Nancy Arrowood

WOODSONG
P U B L I S H I N G

Seymour, IN

Cause For Joy
A Book of Christmas Stories

Nancy R. Arrowood

2016

Scripture quotations are from the King James Version of the Bible.

Woodsong Publishing
5989 Spring Meadow Lane
Seymour, IN 47274

Woodsong books can be ordered at:
www.woodsongpublishing.com

Woodsong books may also be ordered through various retailers.

Cover design by Vision Graphics

Printed in the United States of America

ISBN 978-0-9979146-1-0

Dedicated to

Matthew
Zion
Lucia
Audrey
Mimi

Introduction

The goal for a jigsaw puzzle solver is to be able to put all the pieces together. If one piece is missing in the end, the puzzle will always be incomplete. When a person is born, are they given a box of puzzle pieces to be put together? Perhaps the pieces we are given can be put together in more than one way. Maybe we decide what picture will appear by our attitudes, choices, and people we know and love.

Life may also be like a completed puzzle, with the passing of years removing pieces. So, in the end—instead of a perfect puzzle—we discover more and more pieces are missing as a result of family members passing away, their part of the picture of who we are, gone.

This change, often viewed as loss, forces us to evaluate what really matters most in our living. As pieces—people—are removed from our puzzle through death and various circumstances, we begin to see more fully and clearly that:

Family members are treasures.
Shared experiences are treasures.
Holidays and holiday traditions are treasures.
It is God's gift for us to be alerted to their importance before these treasures are lost.

Christmas 1968 was a holiday of enlightenment. I experienced an awakening that particular Christmas when I spent the holiday alone, several states away from my family. I discovered—like an epiphany—how much family matters. Fast forward the scene. Of my growing-up household, my Great Aunt Ruth, Dad, Mom, and my sisters Cleo and Barbara have passed on. Only my sister Deborah and I remain.

Beginning in 1997, the year our Mother left us, I began trying to capture moments in writing to share with my children. Life seemed to be sifting through my fingers like sand, and I felt perhaps I could retain some of it by recording thoughts, experiences, traditions, and moments with those I loved. Oral stories are great, but those important fragments—experiences dear to my heart, or lessons learned—were going to be lost forever if I didn't record them for my children and eventually grandchildren. I believe moments and memories are the colors and hues that pull life out of the flat, black and white print of obituaries. People do more than just be born and die. In fact, we have little to say about those two events. But the in between, ahhhh…there is the substance, the purpose, and the love we give and take that makes life worth living.

Thus began a new tradition—an annual Christmas message—that I could pass along. This short book is a compilation of those messages. It is my sincere desire that they be enjoyed and serve as a reminder to all of us that Christmas is "A Cause for Joy."

Nancy R. Arrowood

Cause for Joy

For unto us a child is born, unto us a son is given:
...and His name shall be called Wonderful, Counsellor, The
mighty God, The everlasting Father, The Prince of Peace.
Isaiah 9:6

Swirling about me are memories in snow-globes. As I pluck each one from the air, the scenes begin to take shape. I dive into each picture and join in the laughter and singing of cherished holidays of the past. Suddenly the laughter evaporates as the reality sets in that some loved ones are gone, and I will never share Christmas with them again. I cry as if they left just yesterday.

It is self-centered reminiscing, and although it hurts, I journey on. However, someplace along the way I stub my toe. I grab it up, hopping on one leg. I moan with pain and self-pity. But it is only then that I see the Inn Keeper of that first Christmas, and he has my face! Have I become so occupied with the busyness of Christmas—gift buying, decorating, meal planning, and even memory chasing—that I have neglected to think why this holiday began?

Shhhhhh... Is that Jesus knocking softly on my holly-decorated door? Turning the knob and peering out, the cold wind of truth blows in. Will it take an angelic interruption to remind me, or will I just look up like the wise men and begin to search Him out?

1

Cause for Joy

Of those who came that first Christmas, I want to be like the wise men. They left cozy homes and traveled long, through perilous lands, to find Him. Why did they make the journey? What burning desire kept them on the trail? They came to bring gifts to show Him honor and to worship Him. That was all. It was never about them! What did they know of His coming? It is slim chance they knew Jesus had come to die for the world. An attitude adjustment is needed. It squeaks in resistance as I push self out of the way.

Jesus, I have come to marvel at the manger. This Christmas, however, just above it, I see a cross lighting up the sky, instead of a star. I offer afresh my paltry self. All else I have are Your gifts to me. I am kneeling in awe, looking at your baby face but adoring You as my Savior. You are my cause for joy and reason for rejoicing.

Place for a Crippled Duck

To whom God would make known what is the riches of the
Glory of this mystery among the Gentiles:
Which is Christ in you, the hope of glory.
Colossians 1:27

I can't remember how it happened, but somehow it did. Two ducklings, yellow and noisy, but one had a crippled leg. One duck waddled nonchalantly around the barnyard, accepted and confident. The other duck struggled to just get food and water. A duck's body isn't made for navigating around on one leg. So wherever he tried to go, it was with much awkward flopping.

To make matters worse our crippled duck was constantly picked on by the other fowls. The roosters, even the Bantam, especially took delight in pecking him, to the point that his head was plucked bald. He was an outcast of the barnyard society.

Plans for a Christmas meal made an opportunity for Mom and Dad to send him to duck heaven but for the pleas of my sister Barb. She loved our poor crippled duck, and it appeared the feelings were mutual. When Barb would go to the hen house and call "Here, Ducky, Ducky!" that crippled duck would do everything he could to maneuver himself to her. It didn't matter to her that he wasn't graceful. She giggled with delight at his comical efforts but then gathered him

3

up in her arms and lovingly nestled him close. She would make certain he had ample food and water, sometimes even catching a tender bug or two for him to eat.

In the woods near our house meandered a shallow stream flowing from a small pool fed by an underground spring. One day it occurred to us that our ducks might like to go for a swim. We wondered if it would be safe for our crippled duck, but there was only one way to find out. What a transformation happened before our very eyes! It was like seeing a miracle. Once in the water our crippled duck looked just like a normal duck. Instead of his head bent with awkward flopping, his head was held as erect and proud as the other duckling.

I cherish my memories of that day, because in the years that followed, I realized I was more like that crippled duck than the one that was whole. Oh, both my legs worked fine, but deep inside of me there was brokenness. My brokenness made me feel awkward and somewhat an outcast. I was fearful and questioned love, until I found my place in the Christmas story.

I have traveled to Bethlehem many times with Mary and Joseph. I have felt the chill and the weariness as they searched for shelter. I have watched with awe but sympathy, too, that there was only a barn available. Life appeared too hard until I understood God's purpose.

In Bible days shepherding was one of the lowest rungs on the social ladder. It was reserved for those who didn't have any other trade. Yet, Gabriel's angelic host made their holy announcement first to shepherds. If Jesus had been born anywhere other than a stable, the shepherds and their flocks would not have been welcome.

Jesus' ministry began that first night while He was yet wrapped in swaddling clothes and lying in a manger. The lowly shepherds, possibly with their self-esteem plucked away, came to a barn and knelt. They came with empty arms but found His outstretched. Their awkwardness vanished as they discovered the One whose gift is value, respect, and love in place of their brokenness. They could walk away with their heads held high. Jesus came to the lowest first so that all would know it's not about what you have but what's in your heart.

The Christmas message is still applicable for us today. Look back at a stable. Peer into the eyes of a baby and see a cross. Listen to His coos and hear Him cry, "It is finished!" Feel the love and compassion that brought Him. Leave your brokenness at His feet and walk away in newness of life. Jesus' birth and life are proof that He came to make a place for all the broken people of the world. And, if we are honest with ourselves, we are all broken and in need of a Savior.

An Angel's Perspective

And the angel said unto them, Fear not: for, behold,
I bring you good tidings of great joy,
Luke 2:10

Christmas 1976 came at a very lean time in the Arrowood house. With no money for gifts, I recycled some toys belonging to our two young sons. I consoled myself that the fun for children was in unwrapping. That thought soothed a little but not quite enough to lift me to the holly-jolly stage.

I didn't have a lot of tree decorations, but it became very important to me to make the tree as pretty as possible with what I had. Our four-year old, Andrew, responded as if it was the most beautiful tree of all times. Overwhelmed with temptation to touch and explore the shiny ornaments, he turned the tree over twice. I resigned myself to a messy, lop-sided tree but none too happily. I was soaking in a stinky pot of my own self-pity, and it put a damper on my holiday spirit.

Our one-year old, Aaron, was too young to know, but Andrew didn't seem to mind slightly used toys. I was touched by their joy, but I watched standing on the outside looking in. No joy reflected in me. Angry and disappointed with life, my perspective was as lop-sided as my ruined tree. I didn't stop to consider that Mary and Joseph's Christmas was anything but perfect; yet, there was cause for great joy that first Christmas.

An Angel's Perspective

Christmas joy can be elusive. Joy has to do with perspective. It doesn't come from getting the right presents, bright decorations, or even generous amounts of one's favorite cookies. The phrase, "Jesus is the reason for the season," has become a little worn, but none-the-less, it is still true. The angels filled with joy that first Christmas were bursting to tell somebody. They couldn't wait till morning, so they found some working the night shift. The shepherds, watching their flocks by night, were the first to hear the angel of the Lord proclaim, "Behold, I bring you good tidings of great joy, which shall be to all people!" From the angels' perspective the greatest event in history had just taken place, no matter that it transpired in a lowly stable, amid animals, straw, and dung.

Life is full of challenges, some good, and some not, and others some place in between. The difference often depends on one's perspective. So, no matter how lean a Christmas may be, recalling that first Christmas and what it means for us today, it is important to keep "An Angel's Perspective." Their perspective is the source of exuberant joy. Go ahead. It's okay. The Savior is born! Be happy!

Christmas Choices

Some blame the innkeeper for the scratchy straw and drafty barn. It seems absurd that God—who determined before time to confine His flesh to a single cell—was born accidentally in a barn. Certainly He chose His birthplace. Nothing about that first Christmas was an accident or coincidence. Christmas unfolding as it did was His choice. Christmas continues to offer choices—yours and mine.

Eve's catastrophic decision caused chaos; Mary's decision brought order. Eve's choice birthed jealousy, hate, anger, cruelty, and suffering; conversely, through Mary's young womb came self-sacrifice, peace, love, and hope.

Christmas is a story of wonder and hope restored. From the straw bed and barn stench, order emerged. Jesus came to heal the wound Eve's self-centeredness created. He is crushed that we might live. He is slain that we may have wholeness and newness of life.

For many, Christmas is celebrated like Eve's "what-do-I-want" attitude. Instead of Mary's "what-does-God-want" submission.

Christmas Choices

Eve chose her will above God's. She birthed a son full of jealousy and hate. Mary chose God's will above her own. She birthed a son full of compassion and love.

Eve chose her will and lost Eden's paradise. Mary gave up her will to receive eternal life. Eve's son slew his brother. Mary's son laid down His life for others. Eve's choice hurt all of us. Mary's choice blessed all of us.

Listening to Christmas music, my soul is stirred in amazement of God's coming to earth. Lord, how did such a thought come to You of confining Your flesh to a single cell? You understood the body has five million sensory points, each capable of transmitting pain. You were aware that hands have over two million sensory points, and yet, You spread Yours wide for nails. Perhaps even more amazing, You fully realized the mental and emotional anguish of being rejected and despised by those You were dying to save.

Jesus, that night in the stable, oblivious to most of humanity, You set in motion Your plan to suffer and die. I am both horrified and thrilled beyond my words to describe.

This Christmas the responsibility is on my shoulders. What will I do knowing Your awesome love? Will I be like Eve and choose my will regardless of Your plan for my life? Will I resist all suffering and choose momentary gratification? Or will I lay my life at Your feet and allow Your will for me to be accomplished? Help me, Lord, to understand that the end result is worth the struggle. What will it be? Can I let my faith eyes see? Am I willing to put my hand in Yours and walk joyfully the path You have chosen for me?

Lord, my heart wants Your will, but my body sometimes gets in the way. I know a little of pain, and it frightens me. As I write, I hear Your words clearly, "Casting all Your care upon Him; for He careth for you" (I Peter 5:7). Cast? Oh, I love Your choice of words! As of this moment there are a lot of cares weighing heavy on my back. You didn't say, "Give me a couple of those." You said, "Cast ALL your cares!" This Christmas I am determining to cast more. The One Who carried my cross will even carry me. Jesus, I choose You.

Christmas Gift

...but the gift of God is eternal life through
Jesus Christ our Lord.
Romans 6:23

What is your favorite Christmas gift of all time? Was it some toy, a bauble, or an experience? Was it lasting, or fleeting? Was it useful, or just for viewing? What truly is a gift that lasts for eternity? Is there such a thing?

I've enjoyed many gifts and relished many a Christmas memory. But I think my favorite gifts were those I gave away. Looking into the eyes of a recipient and seeing joy and surprise is a memorable treasure. Recalling laughter, or squeals of surprise are music. I start long before the Christmas season, searching for what I hope is just the right gift. I like wrapping, too, and I hope no one peaks when I'm not looking. However, once wrapped and placed under the tree, I want my recipients to try and guess what the gifts are by shaking and sniffing. I want them to be as curious and as eager to receive as I am to give. Gift giving is a serious matter to me.

The Christmas story is full of the gleeful giving of the Lord Most High. He started early planning His gift to humanity. In fact, He planned it from the beginning of time. He was so excited that He dropped hints along the way through His Word. His hope being that mankind would anticipate His

Christmas Gift

gift's arrival: be looking for it, perhaps even longing for it. He wrapped His gift in swaddling cloth. The simple wrapping couldn't belie the value of His gift. It was worth everything, more than rubies or gold or anything this world had to offer. I can only imagine His pure pleasure in giving a gift of eternal value—the gift of Himself. The Lord takes gift giving seriously.

Roll the clocks forward a couple thousand years. There is another gift in His planning. This gift is His return. It hasn't been purchased on a whim but with His life's blood. He has prepared a mansion big enough for us all to dwell with Him forevermore. He was excited that first Christmas; so I really can't begin to imagine His excitement now. He is also hoping His children are looking at the skies with anticipation. He wants them to long for Him as He is longing for them. As before, there are hints in His Word. I want to be like one of the wise men …watching, searching, and longing. I want to hear the trumpet and the angels singing, too. I want to adore Him like the shepherds, kneeling at His feet. I'm certain He's checking off the days now. It is soon, very soon. Will the gift of His second return be this Christmas? Jesus really does take gift giving seriously.

A "Bee-zerk" Christmas?

Glory to God in the highest, and on earth
Peace, good will toward men.
Luke 2:14

How fast can bees fly? I suppose I should find out to tell this story properly. Experience has taught me, however, that it is possible to out run them. Well, at least until you come to a fence, that is!

Maybe I should start from the beginning. There was a lovely wooded area near our old, mostly-white farmhouse. The terrain was rather rough but pleasant, with a meandering, spring-fed stream and enough knolls and ravines to challenge the imagination of any twelve-year-old girl with even a smidgen of tomboy. I spent hours in that little plot of woods climbing trees and day dreaming all sorts of big adventures.

One typical, woods-wandering day, I accidentally stirred up a bees' nest—literally. When the bees emerged angrily from their nest, I took off like greased lightning (whatever greased lightning is). I ran ahead of them by a few feet, one or two feet ahead anyhow. I didn't waste much time looking back to check. My best efforts came to an abrupt halt with that fence. My only recourse, I thought, was to "make like a tree" and try to fool those bees. I instantly froze.

The bees were upon me immediately, crawling and buzzing over my eyes and inspecting my ears. I held my nose to protect my nostrils from invasion. It is somewhat a challenge to remain completely still with bees testing you with their stingers. But somehow I did. The bees became bored with my lack of response and left rather quickly, to my relief. I've replayed that experience many times in the years since with a bit of pride. I toughed out the swarm.

Around Christmas, however, I've observed some people-antics that remind me of that angry swarm of bees. For instance, on super sale day after Thanksgiving at one of our large department stores, folks assemble in anxious lines for hours prior to the special six AM opening. When the doors are unlocked the stampede begins. Shoppers rush to get one of the five computers going for $400 and other such advertised, limited-numbered items. People report that items have been jerked out of their hands at this sale, or items have been swiped from their shopping carts. Shoppers seemingly go completely "bee-zerk" to get the things they want.

I wonder if you push and shove to take home the best bargains of the day, how do you report your victory? "I knocked down ten people to get this beauty of a deal!" Somehow the whole spirit of what Christmas is about seems to be lost. How do we wrap selfishness and Christmas in the same package? How did the unselfish birth in a lowly stable become the boon for retailers and over-indulgence of children?

How do we reverse the "bee-zerk" Christmas spending into be-calm, be-glad, be-thankful, and believing tradition it once was? Do we have the fortitude to just stop, to allow the swarm to surround us, and to remain still? Can we take the stings of others poking us with guilt-inducing actions that say, "I really love my kids, so I'm getting them this, and this, and this!" Or, "Only twenty shopping days left to go bee-zerk. So, you better get going—like everyone else!" What would next year's finances look like if we just stopped when we came to that self-imposed fence? I wonder if the peace and joy of God's love revealed that holy night might extend past the twenty-four hour holiday into something we could enjoy all year long?

Christmas Is Present

*For the Son of man is come to seek and to save
that which was lost.*
Luke 19:10

Christmas! What an awesome time of year! It is a special time for remembering. It is about surprises and expressions of love for those dearest to our hearts. It is a holiday bedecked with colors, sounds, tastes, and memories.

Traditionally, many Americans decorate their homes with lights, tinsel, and a tree. That is true in my home, too. In fact, whenever we have considered purchasing a home, I've checked to see if there was ample storage space for my Christmas decorations. That is an issue because my Christmas decorations fill ten huge containers!

It is at least a two-day task to unpack my Christmas ornaments and decorate the tree and house. I gingerly unwrap the tin-foil bells my son, Andrew, made in kindergarten over thirty-five years ago. (Andrew also painted a wooden cat ornament hot pink. I always hang it on the backside of the tree. But that is another story.) Then I hang the angels my younger son, Aaron, purchased for me in second grade. These things aren't just decorations or ornaments; they are more like old friends who whisper to me of by-gone years and events our family shared.

Christmas Is Present

One favorite piece is a small olive wood nativity set my husband purchased in Bethlehem in 1982. I caress it gently and think about that first Christmas, the story of Mary, Joseph, shepherds, and wise men. I can almost hear the angels and smell the straw. I marvel at how God stepped out of heaven to allow people to see Him, touch Him, and know Him. I feel again the joy and peace the angels proclaimed!

Yes, Christmas is about memories, some dusty with age. But stop! The story is ever new, for that same Jesus is here now—right now. His eyes are watching. His ear is cupped to listen. He doesn't mind the reminiscing, but He didn't stay a cute little baby. What are you saying to Him amid your holiday planning? He came to seek and save all who are lost. Christmas is present tense, because the Christ of Christmas is here.

Pig-For-A-Day
A Different Kind of Christmas Story

*Beloved, if God so loved us, we ought also
to love one another.*
I John 4:11

There was an awful grossness to the huge hogs—snorting and snipping at one another around the automatic feeder— as each jostled for what they thought was the best eating bin. Mom and Dad had moved our family to the country and were trying their hand at raising a few pigs. I was twelve, and my younger sisters were ten and seven—three little girls bent on teaching the hogs some manners.

First, we selected a nice board, not too long and not too short. We didn't want the board to be so heavy that it could cause us to topple over into the hog pen, yet, it had to be long enough to carry a nice wallop.

Secondly, we selected a pig-for-the-day. That hog would be allowed to eat to his heart's delight without interference from the other hogs. To ensure our chosen pig's eating plea- sure, we would lean out over the fence, and using the board as a paddle, smack the fanny of any hog that tried to butt in on our selected pig.

Oh the squeals of consternation from the hogs we spanked! Invariably the spanked hogs would blame the hog beside them, biting and rooting them roughly. The hogs never seemed to catch on to the three little girls laughing in glee at the havoc they were causing.

Soon, most of the plump white behinds had a rosy blush, but sad to say, no amount of spanking ever seemed to phase their greedy natures. The disgusting behavior in the hog-eat-hog world seemed to justify all our deviltry. Gluttony and selfishness had completely taken over. It was an ugly sight.

Greed can also get a hold on people. They may erroneously think that looking out for old number one is the avenue to success and maybe even happiness. Like a present-day Scrooge, they spend their days grabbing and grappling for all they can get—more money, more clothes, more things, more pleasure...just more! It is as ugly and disgusting in humans as it is in pigs.

It is also contrary to everything the Bible teaches. Consider:
- God loves a cheerful giver...not cheerful getter.
- Prefer one another...not me first!
- Two coats? Give one away to someone who has none
- Love thy neighbor as thyself.

Christmas is a special time to stop and think of others. There isn't a lot I can do about the needy of the world, but if I can ease the loneliness or despair of one or two that I know about, I believe God will be pleased. And, after all, it is His birthday. He doesn't need food or clothes or even money. What He needs is someone to care about others, like He did by coming that first Christmas.

This December, I want to have more than a pig's mentality. I want to give more than I receive. I want to share instead of being selfish. I want to send joy to the realms of Jesus by living according to His commands and example.

In so doing, maybe I can smell the hay a little better.
- Maybe I can see the glow of a star on fresh snow.
- Maybe I can hear the faraway whisper of the first carol ever sung.
- Maybe I can sense the presence of a baby born for all the world, rich and poor alike.

And maybe, just maybe, I will capture a tiny peek at the awe and wonder of what that first Christmas was all about.

Christmas Commitment

Commit thy way unto the Lord; trust also in him,
And He shall bring it to pass.
Psalm 37:5

The story is old but ever new by the vibrant colors of it: blood red with courage, true blue with faithfulness, and white hot with passion. It began in Nazareth, a small town in northern Palestine. Jerusalem's religious elite considered the Nazarenes (those from Nazareth) sub-par, a bit too influenced by the many irreligious caravans passing through their community. Jerusalem's religious order considered the trampled dung on the streets a reflection of the condition of the inhabitants' hearts. And even some chided, "Can any good thing come out of Nazareth?"

Nazareth may seem an unlikely place for the story to start, however, those of us who know the end of the story are not surprised. Jesus never avoided societies' outcasts. He seemed to find gold where no one else dared look. But let's get back to the beginning of the story.

God entrusted His greatest plan to a teenager, placing His seed of hope in the soft folds of her virgin womb. Mary wasn't a super woman but a tender maiden with the fresh dew of dreams moist upon her cheeks. Who would have imagined that a young woman—already promised in marriage—would put aside her personal plans and goals to fulfill

Christmas Commitment

God's plan? This story must amaze those who choose promiscuity, abortion, divorce, and sometimes estrangement for "personal" happiness. The angel's visit and request came as a surprise, but Mary didn't wrestle with the cost; she didn't fret and fuss with self-pity over the possible distrust of her espoused. The potential for disaster wasn't a roadblock in her decision-making.

How did she do it? How did someone so innocent handle the whispering behind her back? There was no one to mentor her on becoming the mother of God. And Joseph! What young husband today would be willing to abstain from the sacred bed for months that he not pollute the plan of God?

That first Christmas was raw with giving rather than getting. That first Christmas was about commitment. It demands that I ask myself if the colors of my commitment to Christ are also bold and bright. Or have I slipped into the dull shades of half-hearted commitment? Do I begrudgingly sacrifice for Christ, secretly wishing for the pleasures of sin for a season? How cheaply would I sell out, if faced with the wrong temptation? Though young, Mary cut her way through the jungle of pitfalls and decisions of a "me-me-me" society. With trepidation I place myself beside her and ask, would I be willing to give up personal goals for God's calling? Would I leave family behind and travel to a new land, if God should ask it of me? What if my Christian journey would lead me to a stable? Would complaining be my response?

These questions deserve my careful and honest self-evaluation. I hope that Jesus would find in me what He found in Mary—a commitment to Christ that might cost the world but in the end bless me beyond measure and perhaps be a light for those who come after me.

Christmas Because

*For God so loved the world, that He gave His only
Begotten Son that whosoever believeth in Him should not
perish, But have everlasting life.*
John 3:16

All Christianity wholeheartedly agrees that Christmas is all about Jesus. We recall the adages: "Jesus Is the Reason for the Season," and "Let's Keep Christ in Christmas." Yet, of the four gospels, only two record Jesus' birth—Matthew and Luke. Only Matthew shares the account of the wise men.

We don't know if Jesus had blue eyes or brown. We don't know if He was chubby or slim. We don't know if He was a fussy baby or pleasant and sweet.

Luke shares Jesus birth, jumps to eight days later, and then jumps to the account of something He did when He was twelve. Matthew describes His birth and His family's flight to Egypt, but abruptly leaps to His baptism by John. However, all four gospels are packed with Jesus' teaching, His miracles, and His promises! That gives me pause to wonder why?

Perhaps if Jesus would explain, He might say, "Christmas is about you." Then turn and point to those beside you and say, "Oh yes, and you, and you, and you…and your family, and your neighbors, and all the people of the world."

27

Christmas Because

Are you surprised? You shouldn't be. His coming had a purpose beyond Mary posting His baby pictures on Facebook or creating a new holiday. He came so we would know that the God of this universe loves us. His birth was a necessity in order that He could later die for our salvation. In Jesus' heart, Christmas is a worthy celebration because it was His first step to Calvary.

So, you and I can rejoice with the angels...
Kneel with the shepherds...
And worship with the wise men.

Jesus Christ came because you matter. Jesus is saying to all of us, even though it's His birthday, "Christmas is about YOU."

A Christmas Experience

...he that is of a merry heart hath a continual feast.
Proverbs 15:15

I wish everyone could have grown up with a Great-aunt Ruth. She had a way of making every day special. For example, our bedtime toast snack was cut into strips she called, "saw logs." We had no idea why she called them saw logs, but I promise you, saw logs taste so much better than regular toast. Bedtime stories were one of her specialties, too. Just a chapter or two each night of the "Bobbsey Twins" sent us smiling to dreamland.

One idea, though, turned out to be a super disaster. My parents invited all of the young people from our church for a Christmas party at our house. Mother wanted the kids to know what an old-fashioned Christmas was like. We strung popcorn and cranberries for the tree, and made red and green chain garlands from construction paper. Some made paper snowflakes. Aunt Ruth's contribution was home made taffy.

She cooked up a huge batch on the stove. We decided on partners, and Aunt Ruth gave each duo a glob of candy to pull. We sprinkled confectionary sugar on our hands to keep the candy from sticking to them, and that more than once. The young people spread out to do their best at this new "old-time" adventure. The sticky, sugary concoction isn't

A Christmas Experience

really taffy until you stretch and pull it for a good while—thirty to sixty minutes, depending a lot on the excitement.

As things go with young people laughing and goofing off, globs of candy were dropped and picked up to continue to pull; further, we sprinkled the powdered sugar over and over and "all over." In the end, I'm not sure that any of the taffy was safe to eat, but we never gave that a thought back then. It was all a fun Christmas experience.

The next morning we saw the extent of the disaster. There were bits and pieces of taffy in the carpet, on the porch, on the floor, on the furniture—everywhere. However, the days and effort it took to clean up the accidents seem small compared with the fun we had that night. Mom and Aunt Ruth gave us an endearing Christmas experience to cherish in the years to come. Remembering it makes me laugh, yet.

Christmas celebrations are about Jesus first and foremost. But they are also an opportunity to create some very special times with family. It has been said, "The family that laughs together stays together." Why not give our families more than just gifts? Let's give them a "Christmas Experience."

Gifts From A Father's Heart

As the Father hath loved me, so have I loved you:
Continue ye in my love.
John 15:9

Nine pairs of homemade shoes formed a line by the wood-burning stove in the kitchen. Nine little hearts hoped for Christmas gifts while snuggled in their straw-stuffed mattresses in unheated bedrooms. The four little boys dreamed of bicycles and toy trains. The five little girls longed for Flossy dolls and Teddy bears.

Christmas morning dawned, however, as usual, with just a handful of hard candy and an orange placed lovingly in each pair of shoes. The Baldwin children couldn't help but wonder where the jolly man in the red suit was. The one who delivered such wonderful gifts to their classmates had missed their house again? How unfair!

Maybe all those early years of disappointment are why my Dad didn't get the gift-giving, gift-getting fever typical of the holidays. Besides, Dad struggled every winter keeping the bills paid and food on the table. Typically, around November, he would be laid off and not able to go back to work until early spring.

Even though money was tight, one year Dad broke from his usual habit of not buying gifts. All fall I had swooned how

Gifts From A Father's Heart

I would love to have a pair of black leather gloves with silk lining. I wasn't hinting for them, because I never dreamed I could possibly get them. It was just the frivolous wish of a sixteen-year-old girl. To my great delight and surprise, Dad bought the gloves I longed to own. I was very grateful then, but now I realize more than ever what it cost him. I've tried to picture my gruff, rough-looking father at the fancy clothing counter in Artz's Department Store. The process of selection and purchasing was much more formal then. Most items for sale were kept behind glass counters in containers on shelves. A clerk would get the right container down and hold the item for the customer to see. Dad was certainly out of his comfort zone. He would have felt so awkward and out of place but trying to act naturally. I'm amazed that he did it. Those gloves were an expression of his love that he was never able to verbalize. If Dad were alive today, I would hug him tightly, kiss his cheeks, and say what I missed saying while he was alive: "I love you, Dad. I will never forget your special gift and all you've done for me."

It is so easy to be self-centered, accepting others' kindnesses and sacrifices without much thought. My mind travels back to that first Christmas. It was very, very costly for some. It cost Mary's reputation among her peers, but she graciously and willingly carried her savior baby. Joseph lost the respect of his family and neighbors for marrying a girl pregnant out of wedlock. Many speculated on who the father might have been and how foolish and gullible Joseph was. For all of us, all people of all time, they accepted the humiliation of birthing in a cold, stinky barn. The shepherds came and wise men too, but to most they were just a struggling young family not worth a second thought. I would love to tell Mary and Joseph how much I appreciate and admire them. I would like to say, "Mary and Joseph, thank you. You set aside your own dreams and goals for us. We won't forget your sacrificial gifts for all eternity."

Several years ago, Jesus gave me a very special Christmas gift all my own. I had the audacity to ask Him for a gift on HIS birthday! I'm a bit ashamed of that now, but He heard and answered. I had acquired an autoimmune disorder that caused the crippling of my hands. My fingers were twisted and drawn in different directions, making it painful and difficult to use my hands in any way. Four days before Christmas 2011, I awoke with my fingers straight for the first time in months. I wasn't yet well and wouldn't be for some time, but Jesus gave me back my hands for Christmas.

Jesus' birth was just the beginning of His gifts. He made Himself needy to show us how much He cared. He made Himself vulnerable to make our eternal joy possible. He didn't have to come that first Christmas, but He did. He didn't have to direct my steps as a child to Him, but He did. He didn't have to hear my self-centered plea, but He did. From His great heart to my once-crippled hands, He proved His love again.

Dad is gone and will never hear how much I love him this side of glory. But Jesus, my heavenly Father, is listening today. I don't have to wait to lavish Him with my love and appreciation. On Christmas and every day of the year, I want to say, "Jesus, I love you. Thank You for all the gifts from Your heart."

Christmas Lights

The people that walked in darkness have seen a great light:
They that dwell in the land of the shadow of death,
Upon them hath the light shined.
Isaiah 9:2

My husband loves a sunset bursting with beautiful colors of every hue. As darkness comes, the stars appear. He marvels at them and counts them. The blacker the sky, the more stars are distinguishable.

Some fear the night, but darkness is merely the absence of light. Jesus has never been afraid of the darkness. It was into a dark world that He first came. Romans ruled with their myriad of false gods and cruelty. Religious leaders cared more for the prestige—and the coin—than they did truth.

Christ Jesus, the "Great Light," stood in contrast to the power plays and greed. His hands and heart were out-stretched to the lowly and needy. His message of love was not comprehended by some because of the darkness; however, for many, His love shone more brightly because of the surrounding darkness.

Turmoil reigns in our world today. It is very dark. But the blacker the world, the more the "Light" shines. It's not time to be afraid. It's time to look up in expectation. The same

Christmas Lights

God who chose to come to earth two thousand years ago has promised to return.

Interestingly, during the celebration of Jesus' birth, folks decorate their homes with lights. Purposefully or not, it seems symbolic of the light foretold by the prophet Isaiah. My prayer is that we recognize afresh just what that "Light" means.

Finding the Way to the Manger

Now when Jesus was born in Bethlehem of Judea
in the days of Herod the king,
Behold, there came wise men from the east to Jerusalem.
Matthew 2:1

Wise men afar watching….traveling…searching.
   But those next door seemed to miss it.
      Scribes and Pharisees knew the promise,
         But must have thought, "It won't happen today."
Angels stood sentinel with bated breath in anticipation.
   Demons shuddered with dread.
      The most important event of the then world's existence had just happened.
      And most missed it.

Did the muck and struggle of day-by-day living cause the miracle-birth to be missed? Was the innkeeper too busy counting his money? Was his wife too busy changing beds and cooking for guests? Was Mary's mother too busy worrying about what the neighbors were saying? Was her grandmother too embarrassed to believe Mary was innocent?

Whatever the reason, only a few experienced the "glory" of that night. The miracle of that long ago Christmas yet yearns to be captured. We may have to turn off the radio noise of jingle bell songs. We may have to miss the TV specials that ignore the real meaning of Christmas. We may need to consider shopping less, eating less, and looking more. Looking at the story in Scripture. Letting ourselves be transported mentally to kneel in the hay. Reaching out to embrace the message, "Jesus Christ the Savior is born today."

A Christmas Point of View

But seek ye first the kingdom of God,
and His righteousness;
And all these things shall be added unto you.
Matthew 6:33

Christmas. It is the pinnacle from which mankind sees the past, present, and future in a clearer perspective. The story unfolds, and for the first time mankind sees the vision of God take shape. It is the birthing of our salvation: the revelation of how God moves in simple lives to do the miraculous. He dealt with Joseph and Mary in much the same way He deals with all of us. First—a calling. Decision time. Not a slippery slide—but an uphill journey requiring effort, determination, and faith.

Caesar Augustus disrupted the lives of many by demanding the people go to the city of their birth to register for taxes. What a clever scheme! Perhaps Joseph—on the arduous journey from Nazareth to Bethlehem—reflected, "If it is God's will, why isn't the way easier? Why should God's chosen be subjected to a tyrant's arrogance?" He didn't realize he was fulfilling God's prophecy concerning the place of Jesus' birth. So, Mary, nine months pregnant, weary with the weight of her God-baby, trudged over rutted, rock-strewn roads to reach Bethlehem—just in time.

God's will requires faith. I don't know what Joseph expected when he reached Bethlehem, certainly more than stable accommodations for the King of all kings. Were there tears in Mary's eyes as she entered the stable? Did Joseph's heart ache as he cleared away the animal droppings to prepare a makeshift delivery bed? Did they feel forgotten—even forsaken—by the angel messenger who appeared in the beginning? How often has this temptation to doubt been present in our callings, too?

Yet, when Joseph and Mary did all that they humanly could, God stepped out of their shadowy doubts to show Himself mighty. First came the shepherds, exclaiming the tale of angels and music. The wise men arrived with gifts. In retrospect, their visit kept Mary and Joseph encouraged during their exile. Only God knew how much money they were going to need for their flight and exile in Egypt. As is His way, the provision came just in time.

The birth of Jesus was a singular event, but its lessons are repeated. Our callings require much of the same process. We, too, must help shoulder the load through effort and determination. When down to our last resource, we must hold fast in faith to God's promises. When necessary, the Lord will point the way and affirm His promises with the miraculous.

This Christmas, with twinkling lights and packages stacked to the ceiling, let's consider how Christmas first happened and what it required. When carols are sung, let's remember, that same Jesus is with us still. Let's offer Him our gifts of effort, obedience, and faith. What about our impossible situations? At the perfect moment He will intercede, and if necessary, dispatch angels to give us the miraculous. Perhaps we can see our present circumstances a little more clearly through a "Christmas Point of View."

The Gift of Family

And be ye kind one to another, tenderhearted,
Forgiving one another, even as God for Christ's sake
hath forgiven you.
Ephesians 4:32

Snow, snow, and more snow! Sixteen inches of the powdery stuff swirled into drifts two to three feet deep around me. To think I once prayed for snow on Christmas! The temperature dipping to minus seventeen, I felt like the *Little Match Girl* without the matches. I thought for sure my hands would be frostbitten before my bus arrived. If only I could have afforded some gloves, but working for Mr. Shiffer was like working for Scrooge himself. The tin can of peanuts he gave me for Christmas just kept me from being able to keep my hands in my pockets. What a miserly little man! Oh well, it really wasn't his fault I was so miserable.

Ice crystals covered the windows of the bus, inhibiting my view and reminding me how shut-off—or perhaps shut out—I was. Gloomy thoughts pressed me to wonder if I just vanished would anyone notice? But this prison of isolation was my own making, though I never dreamed I would be so lonely. My soul cried for the nearness of someone to touch, to feel the warmness of someone alive. I ached for the sight of eyes looking back in love for me.

I missed all the ordinary things that I once took for granted, like baking pumpkin pies with Mom to the background of

The Gift of Family

Snoopy's Christmas LP—just audible above my sisters' silly chatter and giggling. I missed the harmless teasing and banter around the 5,000-piece jigsaw puzzle on the library table. I especially missed singing Christmas carols with the family gathered around the piano. I actually missed the sound of soft breathing that meant someone was near; ironically, I missed all the sounds I never heard before, when my life was crowded full of the noises of activity. Back before this time, how did I miss the sweetest things, the things I long for now? I didn't realize how precious they were.

When all is stripped away and rawness is exposed, the needs become so simple, so basic. What I longed for were the true riches of this life I previously ignored, or ignorantly overlooked. Those things I thought important appeared meaningless since my vision had been washed clean by tears of grief for what once was. Why couldn't I realize what really mattered before I reached this point? Why didn't I grasp the value of family before I lost it? The sharp shards of broken family that I had left pierced my soul.

These were the unspoken thoughts of my heart December 24, 1968. I existed—to say lived would be stretching it—in St. Paul, Minnesota. My family lived in Upper Sandusky, Ohio, seven hundred miles away. Petty differences and conflicts robbed me, and like a sneak thief, my treasures were stolen while in a sense I slept, blinded by pride and resentment. That was forty-eight years ago, but the lessons I learned in my loneliest Christmas have never left me.

Out of my heartache a desire was birthed to love and cling to my family, no matter what, and to also be aware of others around me who may need love the way I did my first Christmas in St. Paul. So, I buy gifts for all kinds of people, send cards and notes to people I never hear from, and invite folks with no near family to my home. It may look foolish to those who have never spent Christmas alone, but it is my "Gift of Family" for anyone who wants it.

I believe Jesus smiles when we care about others, especially on His birthday. What's a birthday party without others? Perhaps that's why angels sent shepherds to a lonely stable in Bethlehem. In essence, the angels were saying, "Mary, Joseph, and Jesus all alone? No, no, no! Let's start this Christmas business out right. Let's include others in our celebration!" I guess the Lord Himself was the first to enjoy the tradition of the "Gift of Family."

God's Messy Christmas Gift

...The angel of the Lord appeared unto him in a dream
saying, Joseph, thou son of David,
fear not to take unto thee Mary thy wife:
for that which is conceived in her is of the Holy Ghost.
Matthew 1:20

Some expanding. Some aching.
　　Some "oh my-ing." Some moaning.
　　　　But then…some smiling. Some sighing.
Some spit-up and diapering.
　　Some colic and burping.
　　　　Funny thing about babies…they are soooo messy!

God blessed me with two. Andrew came first. Three years later came Aaron. When Aaron was a couple months old, Andrew climbed into his crib. Somehow he managed to climb back out with his baby brother in tow. By the time I discovered what was happening, Andrew had Aaron in his arms and was rocking him in his teddy bear chair. I really can't imagine the maneuvers required to accomplish that feat! There ensued several other escapades that made me thankful Aaron survived. Babies can be so unpredictable— so messy!

Of all the ways and places to present the world with His only begotten son, the Lord chose the messy way.
- Young, unwed mother—had all the neighbors talking.

- Crowded, cramped city—no room for one more couple.
- Lowly, animal-scented stable—just swaddling cloth for clothing.

It appeared so haphazard, so messy. But for angels, shepherds, and wise men who saw beyond the messy, it was a gift beyond description.

There are a lot of messy things in this world—little children without fathers, fathers without jobs, mothers without patience. Not enough money. Not enough energy. Not enough hope. It is just in such an environment that the Lord steps in. He isn't afraid of the messy. He understands because He came the messy way with a message for each of us. He wants everyone to realize this Christmas, "I love you. I came the messy way so you would know."

Christmas Memories

But, beloved, remember ye the words which were spoken
Before of the apostles of our Lord Jesus Christ;
Jude 1:17

Sweet memories dance around in my head like sugarplums in the beloved old poem. Each scene fills me with wonder. I see smiling faces, hear the giggles, and smell the aromas of vanilla, cinnamon, and whiffs of pine.

Each happy memory parades before me in a line. "Little Drummer Boy" keeps time. I am lifted up in the beat into a rising spiral of joy. I laugh with Mom, Dad, and Aunt Ruth at the silly antics of my little sisters. I sit at the piano and play carols with family singing—on and off key—around me. Funny how I took it all for granted way back then.

Eventually the memories carry me to those spots—the ones I shrink from because they are empty. Some may think people are replaced as they depart, but that never happens. We go, on and though years soften the pain, our dear ones are never replaced. Perhaps that may happen with pets but NOT people. Like a weary traveler I realize it is time to go home—back to the here and now of reality—to the present.

Very carefully I pluck each memory from the air and re-wrap it. I handle each one gently so not to damage it or cause it to loose any of its twinkle or sparkle. I determine to guard

Christmas Memories

these memories, like a bulldog his bone, that I might savor them again next Christmas.

A tear threatens to escape my eye when the door suddenly swings open. To my delight my grandson pops into the room, all energy and enthusiasm. He has come to help me decorate the tree with baubles and dangles kept from a lifetime of Christmases. He has no idea how it delights me when he asks, "Where is your red bell, Grandma?" Or, "Where is the angel for on top of the tree?" The past fades a little as the present marches boldly and joyfully into my heart.

Toys come and go. The ones he longs for today will be discarded as he grows older and moves on to other things. I'm hoping, as I did, he is forming pictures in his mind. They are the treasures I want him to hold and enjoy after I'm gone. And perhaps someday, like me, he'll reminisce about the good times and write his stories for his children.

His Unspeakable Gift

Thanks be unto God for His unspeakable gift.
II Corinthians 9:15

His feet ached with weariness as he shuffled along the dusty road. But concern for his wife crowded out any thoughts of self-pity. They were both exhausted and in need of shelter. The three-day, ninety-mile trek from Nazareth had taken its toll. Worse, from all indications, the birth of their special child was imminent. They needed shelter, immediately.

Once again, thoughts of the angelic visit momentarily carried Joseph away. Awe beyond imagination swelled in his chest. "How could his sweet, young Mary actually be the chosen mother of the promised Messiah?" He pondered. The doubts and disdain of his family and hers, had cut deep, but nothing could steal the joy of the promised babe's arrival. "What an honor that he, a simple carpenter, would be the step-father of God's greatest gift to mankind!" It all seemed too grand and glorious to be true. But it was true.

He stumbled slightly but caught himself. Up there, just ahead, he saw flickering candle-lights and a rough sign indicating Bethlehem's Inn. He imagined how delighted the innkeeper would be to help them. "Hold on, Mary, I will soon have a warm bed for you."

"No room! What? This can't be happening! Mary! Mary! I am so sorry," Joseph lamented. "I never thought it would be like this. I wanted better for you. It seems our holy baby, the Lamb of God, is destined to be born in a stable, just like an ordinary lamb."

Today our celebrations of Christmas hold little semblance of that first Christmas. We sit in cozy homes filled with the aromas of delicious foods. We laugh with family and share special Christmas's of the past. Too often, perhaps, it is more a celebration of us than of Him.

Yet, I don't believe Jesus wants us to spend a night in a barn in remembrance of Him. What He chose for Himself was a path of humility. He came in a manner that the poorest would know they were welcome. Lowly shepherds were at ease in His presence. No apologies necessary for the smells of herding. His coming was a gift of love in every way.

Tears well in my eyes at the thought of any hardship Jesus, or His parents, faced. Any cold or hunger or distress they felt grieves me. But He isn't interested in my pity. He gladly suffered all. It is a miracle beyond my imagination, as great as the star that stood sentinel over a stable, as true as the blood that flowed freely down a rough wooden cross, and as glorious as the ascension. From splendor to a stable He pointed the way. From a cradle to a cross He provided the way. Thanks be unto Jesus for His unspeakable gift.

I'll Be Home for Christmas

Peace I leave with you, my peace I give unto you:
Not as the world giveth, Give I unto you. Let not your heart
be troubled, neither let it be afraid.
John 14:27

No matter if it's July or December, the song, "I'll Be Home For Christmas," makes me cry. It started with my fear of losing my Mother, dreading the thoughts of Christmas celebrations without her. She left me nineteen Christmases back, and I'm still missing her. Since loosing her, there's been a bit (probably a lot) of self-pity related to that song.

However, this year I have determined to look back joyfully. I have so many wonderful memories. I've decided to dust them off and cherish them while making new. I'm remembering making snow angels and snowmen. I'm remembering red noses and cold toes after ice-skating. I'm remembering the warmth of Mother's arms and her tender kisses. I'm remembering the twinkle in her eyes as we opened our presents, and I'm remembering her joy when we expressed our pleasure. I'm remembering her laughter when she had kept us from guessing what was in our wrapped gifts. What a treasury of happy memories I have to draw from.

I'm not going to get stuck in the past and miss the joys God has given me today and in my future. I picture the faces of my dearest loved ones. Who can be sad with five grandchildren bouncing around them? How can I be sad with sons and their beautiful wives to laugh with at the antics of the children?

I don't want to be numb this year with glum thoughts of those I miss. I want to be alive and sensitive to all I have left. I want to see the lights, hear the music, taste the cookies, and most of all I want to feel the spirit of Christmas. It is all about the most precious gift of love God could give. Jesus wasn't just a gift for Mary and Joseph or even for the people of Israel. He came because of a love beyond comparison for all of us down through the centuries. He came because He loved me and because He loved all people of all time.

As I relish memories of my Christmases past, I also wonder about the first. I think of Mary and Joseph that chilly night, alone in a stable, no mention of parents or friends. Were they hungry and tired? Were they frightened? Did it bother Mary that a swaddling cloth was the only garment she had for the Christ-child? I'm certain she would have welcomed her mother to comfort and encourage her during labor pains.

But sad thoughts were chased away with the hallelujah chorus of an angelic host that sent their first visitors, the shepherds. Their surprise visit must have reinforced God's promises. Then the wise men's knock! And their special gifts!

My special times aren't over; they are developing in the unfolding Christmases I spend with my children and grandchildren. Whether near, or far, my family is always close in my mind, my heart, and in my prayers. Jesus is their gift too—the best gift there ever was or will be.

My New Christmas List

Verily I say unto you,
Inasmuch as ye have done it unto one of the least Of these
my brethren, ye have done it unto me,
Matthew 25:40

My younger sisters' silly giggles blended pleasantly with Snoopy's Christmas album playing in the background. The Red Baron wasn't the only one moved by the sentiment of the season. Mom had announced it was time to make our Christmas lists, and we were gaga with the thought of brightly wrapped gifts piled under the tree. We were to list five things we would most like to have. That was the hard part. We had visions of all kinds of wonderful things floating around in our heads. That year I wanted an electric razor, because I thought being a teen I should shave my legs. Most of all, however, I wanted clothes. By mid-year the few school outfits I had gotten at the beginning of the year were looking a bit shabby—at least to me.

It was Christmas 1964—the year Dad had his first heart attack. He was only forty-two and it seemed impossible but sadly true. It had been several months since he had been able to work, and money was scarce. Mom had great intentions to make Christmas special, but scramble as hard as she could, she wasn't able to scrape up much in the way of gifts.

I remember hiding, after opening our sparse gifts, and crying broken-heartedly. I tried to keep a brave face for Mom, but inside I was aching. I kept thinking about the first day of school after Christmas break. All my schoolmates would be wearing their new clothes and relating all the gifts they had received. I blushed with humiliation just thinking about being there with nothing new and no stories to share.

I'm embarrassed today to recall my attitude. But how was a teenager to know she had some of the best gifts God ever created: her mother, love of family, her youth, and her health? Ah-h-h now in my late sixties, how I would embrace all of those gifts—gifts I took for granted—and feel like the most blessed person alive. However, at sixteen, I was a bit confused about the reason for the season.

Quite in contrast that first Christmas, the angels weren't confused about which song to sing. Their anthem rang out, "Glory to God in the Highest!" *Up On The Housetop* never was considered in their repertoire.

That first Christmas, the shepherds weren't confused about whom to worship. Their earnest desire was to see God's greatest gift to mankind. A baby in a manger had their full attention. A tree with shiny baubles and lights, no matter how bright and beautiful, could never compare to seeing the face of God.

That first Christmas, the wise men weren't confused in their journey. They didn't come to a humble stable to "get" something. They came to give honor and gifts fit for a king. Little did they realize, baby Jesus had come to give them the gift of eternal life.

With all the hoopla about Christmas decorating and gift giving, it is possible to miss the real meaning of this holiday. In fact, making out my lists for grandbabies and those I love, this year it suddenly dawned on me, "I wonder what Jesus wants for Christmas?" I was surprised to realize that I had not considered that thought before, or even first for that matter.

The Lord is self-sufficient, but I believe these three simple gifts would make the top of His wish list. By His grace I want to cheerfully and reverently present these gifts to Him:

- Express my love to Him. It is the first commandment (Matthew 22:37).
- Offer up appreciation to Him for coming that first Christmas and for all His goodness all year long (Psalm 50:14).
- Follow His example and care for those in need (Psalm 41:1).

By cheerfully and reverently presenting these gifts, I am hoping to make Jesus' Christmas brighter and more beautiful this year.

Why Christmas?

But when the fullness of time was come,
God sent forth His Son, made of a woman…
Galatians 4:4

Have you ever tried to give a rabbit mouth-to-mouth resuscitation? Have you ever hunted live bugs to feed a chameleon? Have you ever nursed a runt pig with a doll baby bottle? Have you ever rode a snow horse until your fanny was frozen? I have.

Sometimes I wonder about myself and ask the big question: "Why?" But I haven't yet come up with an answer. I finally decided it just seemed the right thing to do at the time.

God isn't like that. You can bet your best booties that there is a purpose in everything that He does, that He allows, and that He has planned.

That first Christmas had been in His planning from the beginning. When was the beginning you may ask? Well, only God knows the answer to that. Because He is so beyond time and space, we can't begin to imagine.

Aren't you a little surprised why He chose Bethlehem? Why not Jerusalem? There was a reason. Why a stable and not a palace? I can guess, but why really is obscure to me.

Biggest puzzle of all: Why did He love us so much to come to earth? Flesh, blood, and bones…worthy of His great suf-

Why Christmas?

fering? Whatever His reasons, the fact is plain, He did and still does love us. I hope everyone will take some time to reflect and thank Him. Let's remember the Christ of Christmas.

Christmas in Blue

While we look not at the things which are seen,
But at the things which are not seen:
For the things which are seen are temporal;
But the things which are not seen are eternal.
II Corinthians 4:18

Christmas in California! This is a new experience, moving in on the kids to celebrate the holidays, instead of their coming to our home. No matter how hard they try to make us welcome, I still feel somewhat in the way. I keep trying to push those thoughts out, but they hide, lurking in the corners of my heart and pouncing out at the least hint of boredom with us.

California, the climate, the lifestyle, and the teams of busy people! Somehow I feel we midwesterners just don't measure up—not important enough, smart enough, or perhaps too old-fashioned. It's an adjustment, and it's awkward.

There's a beautiful blue ocean crashing and rolling outside the window of our hotel. The blue swells stretch before me, and with my vision they are endless. Yet, I know they do end, and land begins again somewhere. Life is like that, too. It seems things will go on and on the way they are and never change, but there is an end and a new beginning. Though the waves hump, then splash upon the shore, seemingly to do so for eternity, cataclysmic events can alter them. Events such as earthquakes and hurricanes and sudden unavoidable changes happen.

Christmas in Blue

Day by day we live, eat and breathe. The rhythm of life seems perpetual. Then an event happens that changes everything. We have sons and daughters, and for years they are ours. Then one day they are gone with the simple phrase, "I do." No longer are we the center of their lives but the edge. It hurts if we allow it or fight the change.

How enlightening this experience! Suddenly with keen understanding we realize what our parents felt before us, and theirs before them. We have reached the end of our ocean. We have arrived on virgin soil and must explore new land. We are forced to travel on without the daily companionship of our children. They are charting their own course. They have set sail on their blue ocean.

They visit from time to time, but a major event has taken place, and our lives are forever changed. After just a few short days they miss their own homes. They are now on their own journey; we must continue ours. We are forced to re-pack, allowing some things to be left behind. We are forced to re-think the remainder of our years. We are back to the original three: Jesus, Larry, and me. But that's the way it should be, for we prepared them for this journey. I suppose we just didn't prepare ourselves.

Jesus. He has remained a constant in all of this journey. He waited while we so wholeheartedly chased rainbows that only existed in our minds. He patiently paced the waiting room as we labored in childbearing and child rearing. He smiled and stood by as we launched our kids, knowing the course of life. He knew all along about this dawning, this awakening.

I become reflective and wonder if my actions or attitudes ever hurt Him? Did He ever feel left out or left behind in

60

our plans? Did I ever seem impatient or bored with His presence? I know His feelings aren't fragile, because He is the Mighty God. But, He does have feelings. If we have been made in His likeness, rejection or neglect stings Him, too. I am afraid too often I have been the center of my own universe instead of reserving that place for Him alone.

Like a burst of great light—coming out of the darkness—momentarily blinds and then is enjoyed, we see what life is really all about: certainly not money or possessions; not education and being viewed as successful by peers; not beauty, because we see it is fading quickly. No. Not any of those "temporary" things. Life is about being ready to spend eternity with the One who never changes. Today, all is a pale and fragile vapor compared with what is left to come. If my past years were all there was, would not life be miserable? But in His infinite wisdom and generous mercy, He has planned for us a new life. I gaze, but now with eyes adjusted to the additional light, for that approaching shore just beyond this blue ocean.

Waiting for Christmas

The LORD thy God in the midst of thee is mighty:
He will save, He will rejoice over thee with joy:
He will rest in His love, He will joy over you with singing.
Zephaniah 3:17

Christmas crept in on snail feet in 1957. Ugh! I hate waiting! When, oh when, will Christmas get here? From September on, children in my younger years longed for Christmas. Life was a little different then. In those days Toys'R Us would have gone out of business because children seldom received gifts, let alone toys, except at Christmas. School clothes and one pair of school shoes had to last nine months. The only addition was at Christmas, with perhaps a new sweater, or in the more abundant years, a whole outfit!

I discovered early that there really wasn't a Santa. Oh, how disappointed I was! That meant we could only rely on receiving the gifts my Mother could scrape together for us. We were blessed that she always tried to give us some Christmas surprises and happy times with extra special treats to eat. She would make peanut butter fudge, bake a pumpkin pie, and roast a capon complete with her especially moist, sage-free dressing. A 5,000-piece jigsaw puzzle took the whole Christmas break to complete.

Later, there were the years of Mother's sickness. One of her last prayers was that the Lord would allow her to go Christmas shopping one last time and purchase a gift for each of her four girls. There was hope in her eyes, as always, that we would be totally surprised and delighted with our gifts. Amputations had taken both of her legs, and basically, she was waiting to die that Christmas. Actually, she was yearning to pass over to the other side. Knowing how she felt softens the pain in the memories of our last Christmas together.

Yet, I don't believe anyone's longing for Christmas can compare to the Lord's longing for that first Christmas. Before time began He had planned for this event. His anticipation and excitement probably sent shooting stars throughout the heavens. One super bright star pointed to the birthplace for those seeking Him. His longing to be among us, almost as one of us, was so great! His supernatural birth was an expression of His awesome love for us.

For the first time, His face would feel a loving mother's moist kiss. He would know how it felt to be nestled, caressed, and have lullabies sung to Him. He would also experience those human feelings of pain, hunger, and the need for sleep. I'm certain His excitement could not be measured within the limits of human body and mind. This was the culmination of His desire to rub shoulders with His creation like never before. To be known. Those He loved would see His face, touch His hands, receive His gaze, and hear His voice.

An infant cradled in His mother's arms, yet all knowing, therefore, hearing the angels' announcement and joyful song. This God-child knew the shepherds by name, and the hairs of their heads were numbered. But He chose to be confined in His new baby body and receive their humble adoration. He saw past the stable in His God-eyes to cheer for the Magi following the star He had placed in the sky for them.

I can't help but believe His joy was immeasurable. He was here! This was it! The centuries of planning rolled by as He had waited for the fullness of time. He loved the wise men's kind gifts, for they expressed their desire to honor Him. They could not have imagined the golden streets of glory He had left behind to receive their small gift of gold. But none of it was lost on Him. He received their gifts with thankfulness as He received the widow's two mites years later, and today, each child's pennies in Sunday school. It isn't about the size of the gift but about the love behind the giving of it.

I sincerely hope He isn't having to wait on you this Christmas to choose a path of following Him. He might be getting impatient waiting, because He's been waiting quite a while to return to earth for His bride. His joy of that coming event cannot be measured, nor ours either. For the first time we will be able to behold His "glorified" face. Nothing will ever separate us again. With our adoration we will be able to touch His hands and kiss His cheeks. He will literally embrace us and sing over us His songs of love. He is longing for it, waiting for that great day.

Are you earnestly longing for that day too? If not, make this Christmas a celebration of fellowship with Him. Better still, don't make Him wait for Christmas. Make that decision today, and every day.

The Candle

Ye are the light of the world.
Matthew 5:14

One of my favorite events of the Christmas season is watching Christmas programs. The children are darling as many of them recite their lines in shepherd costumes or as fluffy sheep. My granddaughter Lucia's first program cast her as a western girl. She was amazing! Grandma and Grandpa were about to pop their buttons. Truly, though five years old, she recited her lines perfectly with a mix of western and hillbilly accent. She sang her special song with that accent also. I am looking forward to Mimi and Audrey making their debuts. Matthew and Zion are old hands at it now, but each performance is truly a delight.

I remember my first Christmas program, too. I was totally scared out of my brain, but when it was over, my pastor spoke words that I have held in my heart ever since. I'm not certain how old I was, but I know what I wore! I had a new yellow dress and yellow matching sweater. My piece was entitled, "The Candle." After I finished, Pastor Little said, in front of everybody, "That was wonderful, and she looks like a candle, too!" If he were living, he would have a big belly laugh to know how that compliment has stayed with me now sixty plus years. I recall it because it was the first time I remember feeling like I had value.

The Candle

Who sees young children, or any child of any age as far as that goes, as desiring to know they matter. I'm certain I couldn't have articulated that need, but the yearning—though unspoken—was there. It is an empty spot in all of us begging to be filled. After all, aren't adults just children in bigger, older bodies? Every day, we pass people. It is so easy to be task-oriented and miss opportunities to give them the gift of attention.

I've challenged myself to try and see little ones, clerks, waiters, people that I pass, and to try to give to them a little piece of what Pastor Little gave me—words that say they matter. I wouldn't give myself an A+ on the caring chart, but hopefully I see each day as an opportunity to let someone know they have value.

My first recitation was about a candle—a useful tool that shares light. Remembering my pastor's gift to me, and Jesus' gift to all, I am determined to be more of a light to those around me, big or small, by speaking words that reflect the love and light of Christ.

The Wisdom of the Wise Men

When they saw the star,
They rejoiced with exceeding great joy.
Matthew 2:10

Black velvet sky, bright star pointing the way to a lowly stable, shepherds, angels, wise men, and a baby. We've heard it
all before, and if we're not careful, an attitude may form, like:
"I just don't get that much out of Christmas anymore." Did
I say get? When was Christmas about getting? Shouldn't
we be asking, "What did I put into Christmas? What did I
contribute? What did I give?"

Bethlehem of Judea, how blessed you were! But most
missed the opportunity to give on that special night. Was
it because they were all about getting? The innkeeper said,
"No room." He was packed solid with paying guests. This
census thing was quite a boon to his business. He was getting rich. "Getting" was what life was all about for many.
In their drive to get, they missed the chance to give. Born
that day in their midst was God's very best gift. Hmmm....
And, they missed their chance—they didn't recognize the
opportunity knocking on the door.

Someone could have given a hot meal to Mary and Joseph.
Someone could have given a warm place and encouraging
words to a woman in labor. Someone could have given a

soft, clean blanket for the baby. Someone could have given a lullaby to coddle him to sleep.

Some people did think about giving. The wise men noticed a phenomenon in the sky—a star—a very special star. They researched until they discovered that the star announced the birth of a Jewish king. Birthed in their hearts was a desire to go beyond just knowledge of the birth; they determined to seek out His presence.

They saddled their camels and prepared for a long arduous journey. They kissed their wives and children good-bye and set out on a holy quest. Their preparations included gifts. The wise men didn't plan to get something from the new baby; alternatively, they planned to give. They weren't seeking a handout; conversely, they went bearing gifts to give to the newborn King

The wisdom of the wise men is that they went to give rather than to get. They gave their time and effort to search Him out. They traveled far and gave their treasures of gold, frankincense, and myrrh. They gave their adoration and awe, their esteem and honor. The wisdom of the wise men was that they realized Christmas was all about Him. Getting wasn't part of it, but giving was.

That first Christmas others gave too: Mary gave her youth, her body, her blood, sweat, and tears. Joseph gave up his reputation and the esteem of his peers, to stand by Mary when she appeared to have an illegitimate child. The angels gave their song, "Glory to God in the highest!" The shepherds gave their wonder and worship. All these seemed to be thinking about giving—not getting.

Two thousand Christmases have come and gone. It seems

each year the emphasis increasingly is on gift getting and giving to each other, rather than about Him. Is there a way we can change that? Can we look again at the beginning and find a way to give Christ something this Christmas?

With just little thought I realize there are many appropriate gifts: love, trust, obedience, faithfulness, time, praise, my best thoughts, my future, and the list goes on and on. These gifts can't be wrapped in paper and placed under a tree. These gifts are wrapped in the flesh of our hearts. But, gifts of the heart are His favorite.

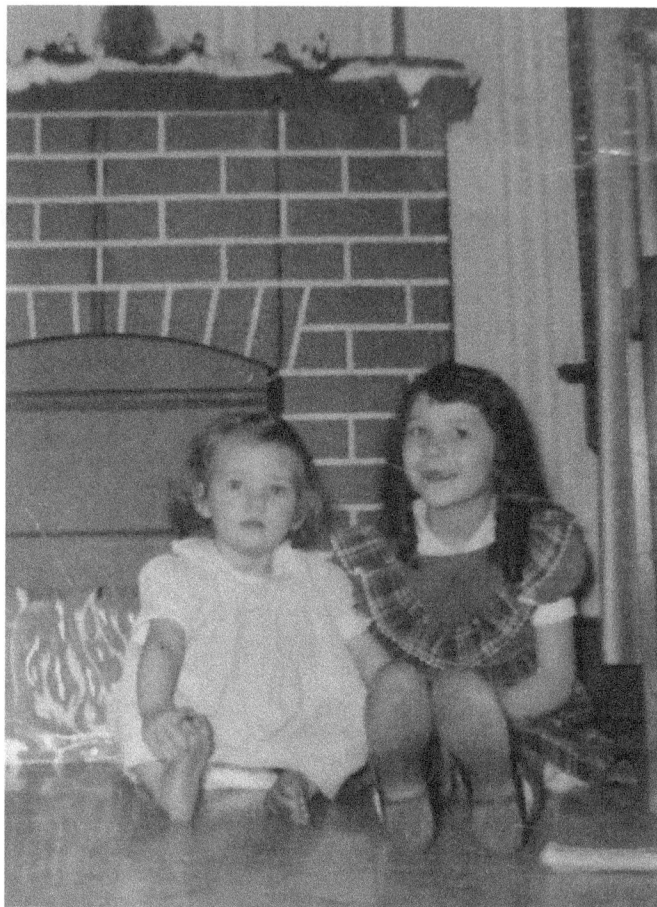

**Nancy and her sister Deb
Christmas 1953**

www.ingramcontent.com/pod-product-compliance
Lightning Source LLC
Chambersburg PA
CBHW031606040426

42452CB00006B/427